FRANK LLOYD WRIGHT'S HOUSE ON KENTUCK KNOB

FRANK LLOYD WRIGHT'S
HOUSE ON KENTUCK KNOB

DONALD HOFFMANN

UNIVERSITY OF PITTSBURGH PRESS

Visiting the House

The house on Kentuck Knob is situated off the Chalk Hill–Ohiopyle
Road, six miles northeast of U.S. 40 in Fayette County, Pennsylvania.
For tour reservations, rates, and information, call (724) 329-1901.

Published by the University of Pittsburgh Press, Pittsburgh, Pa. 15261
Copyright © 2000 by the University of Pittsburgh Press
All rights reserved
Manufactured in the United States of America
Printed on acid-free paper
10 9 8 7 6 5 4 3 2

Library of Congress Cataloging-in-Publication Data
Hoffmann, Donald.
    Frank Lloyd Wright's house on Kentuck Knob / Donald Hoffmann.
        p.   cm.
Includes bibliographical references.
    ISBN 0-8229-4119-8 (cloth : alk. paper)
    1. Wright, Frank Lloyd, 1867–1959—Criticism and interpretation. 2. Architecture,
Domestic—Domestic—Pennsylvania—Fayette County.   I. Title.
    NA737.W7 H623 2000
    728'.373'092—dc21   00-008348

CONTENTS

FOREWORD

Life, on occasion, becomes a matter of serendipity. When circumstances conspire to propel one in a certain direction, it is best to go with the flow, or so I have found, even if the precise destination is at the time unknown.

My purchase of Kentuck Knob in 1986 falls into such a category. A visit to Frank Lloyd Wright's fabled Fallingwater in the company of my eldest daughter, Laura, who was reading history of art, ended with the casual remark from our guide that there was another house by the same architect just down the road; since time was not pressing, why did we not take the opportunity of killing two birds with one stone, as it were?

I went, I saw, and I was conquered—at least from the exterior. The house was unoccupied at the time, and I was unable to gain access to the magical spaces that lay, in my imagination, behind the front door. A second visit was therefore essential, and indeed one was arranged a few weeks later. My ardor burned as bright as ever—brighter still, in fact, when the interior of the house not only met, but exceeded, my expectations. And, thus, the purchase was made.

I think that both I and the State of Pennsylvania owe a great debt of gratitude to Mr. and Mrs. I. N. Hagan for an inspired commission from an architect of legendary renown. The site, moreover, is of a spectacular beauty that never palls whatever the season and whatever the gap between visits, whether one month or ten minutes. The combination of location and design is therefore irresistible to my wife and our children, and we feel enormously privileged to own such a masterpiece and enormously gratified that so many visitors seem to want to come to share our pleasure in the experience of a home that holds, and will always hold, a very special place in our affections.

My feeling of gratitude extends equally to the author of this book, Donald Hoffmann, for a painstaking work of scholarship that is also an immensely good read. I have learned a great deal from his insights

and analysis of this most beautiful and beguiling late work by the hand of the master, and I am sure that all those who read it will do so with a sense of pleasure and delight.

— Peter Palumbo
May 6, 1998

ACKNOWLEDGMENTS

am indebted first of all to Lord Palumbo, of London, who kindly invited me to undertake this study of his house in Pennsylvania, and to Franz Schulze, of Chicago. My visits to Kentuck Knob were invariably happy ones because of the friendly and helpful staff at the site, and I especially wish to thank Susan Waggoner, the director; Marianne Skvarla, curator; and Jon Phelan, Chuck Gall, and Tricia Buzzelli. It was also my good fortune in Pennsylvania to be able to speak with Jesse Wilson of Markleysburg, John Chan of Grindstone, Mrs. Bernardine Hagan of Uniontown, and Bruce Herrington of Rector. For sharing their knowledge of Frank Lloyd Wright's practice in the 1950s, I am grateful to several of his apprentices· Mark

Heyman of St. Louis, John Geiger of Los Angeles, Curtis Besinger of Lawrence, Kansas, and John Ottenheimer of Seattle.

W. Philip Cotton Jr. of St. Louis greatly informed and encouraged this study. I also wish to thank James Baker of New York, Charles F. Eggers of Flagler Beach, Florida, Victoria J. Leonelli, curator of the Pennsylvania Room at the Uniontown Public Library, Monica Ruscil of the Seeley G. Mudd Manuscript Library at Princeton University, Elaine Engst, university archivist at Cornell University, John C. Benyo, assistant director of the Saint Vincent College Library in Latrobe, Pennsylvania, Al Decker of the University Extension Center at Butler, Missouri, Eunice B. Tshabalala of the Forest Products Laboratory in Madison, Wisconsin, Helen Ashmore, also of Madison, Mira Nakashima-Yarnall of New Hope, Pennsylvania, Joel Skvarla of Ohiopyle, Pennsylvania, and my sister-in-law, Kathleen Hoffmann of Springfield, Illinois.

The drawings from Wright's studio and quotations from his correspondence are reproduced by permission of the Frank Lloyd Wright Foundation. I am grateful to Bruce Brooks Pfeiffer, Penny Fowler, Oscar Muñoz, and especially Indira Berndtson of the Frank Lloyd Wright Archives.

For their many years of friendship and encouragement I am indebted to Ellen Goheen, formerly of the Nelson-Atkins Museum of Art in Kansas City, Missouri, and to Edgar Tafel of New York.

— D. H.

FRANK LLOYD WRIGHT'S HOUSE ON KENTUCK KNOB

IN THE MOUNTAINS

Frank Lloyd Wright could not overcome all the claims of old age, but when he sketched Fallingwater, the weekend house above the waterfalls of Bear Run, he was sixty-eight; and when in the winter of 1953–1954 he conceived a splendid house for a nearby site name Kentuck Knob, he was eighty-six. The two mountain houses are thus inevitably compared because of their proximity—seven miles by road, or less than four miles as the crow flies—and as the ripened fruits of Wright's later years. They are also his only buildings in western Pennsylvania.

The relation is closer still. Kentuck, as it is often called, is in a sense the child of Fallingwater. Mr. and Mrs. I. N. Hagan had visited Bear Run on various occasions and had greatly ad-

Fallingwater
(Harold Corsini; courtesy of the Western Pennsylvania Conservancy)

The house on Kentuck Knob

mired Fallingwater before they decided to approach Wright for a house of their own. They wanted a more modest residence, comfortable for two persons, constructed of stone and wood rather than exposed concrete, and with every room on one floor.

Wright said a house should be "a noble consort to man and the trees," and that is exactly what Kentuck became. The house arose from a vital and articulate plan, and it achieved the very qualities Wright praised so many years earlier: dignity, repose, grace, strength, delicacy, severity, and rhythmic order. If it could be regarded as a small house, Kentuck nonetheless spoke to a large vision. It challenged the mind again and again to consider its many aspects, its surprisingly different perspectives.[1]

I. N. Hagan was always addressed by his initials, which led some people to mistake his name for "Ian." He had known Bernardine Landis since childhood, and they had been married in 1930. They lived in an old but substantial house in Uniontown. Hagan was president of the I. N. Hagan Ice Cream Company, which had been founded in 1878 by his grandfather and namesake, who for reasons now forgotten had been named Isaac Newton. The company, headquartered in Union–town, operated branch offices in four other cities and took particular pride in claiming to be the earliest manufacturer of ice cream west of the Allegheny Mountains. The company sold other dairy products as well, and by all accounts, the ice cream was very rich.[2]

Uniontown, the seat of Fayette County, is believed to have taken its name either from the union of real estate parcels that formed the village in 1776 or from the union of states in the War of Independence. In either event, the town is blessed with a magnificent view east toward Chestnut Ridge, which rises more than 1,500 feet above it and stands as the westernmost of the great mountain formations diagonally disposed across so much of Pennsylvania. By itself, however, Uniontown possesses little scenic charm. Its first prothonotary, or clerk of the courts, called the place a little mudhole, and memorably described it in 1783 as "the most obscure spot on the face of the globe." Many improvements were made, of course, but eight generations later, when I. N. Hagan and his wife chose to move to the other side of Chestnut Ridge, fourteen miles from his office, Uniontown was past its heady years of bituminous coal mining and the production of coke for making steel.[3]

The summer of 1953 thus became a time of high excitement for the Hagans. Within a few weeks, they bought a mountain farm, saw their son married, traveled to meet Wright at his home and studio near Spring Green, Wisconsin, and embarked on the adventure of

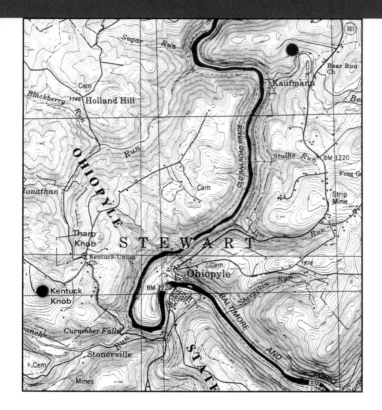

Figure 1. Location of Kentuck Knob (lower left) in relation to Fallingwater (upper right) (Adapted from U.S. Geological Survey map)

engaging his services. To build a house of his design soon became a central purpose in their lives.

In 1953 it was unusual for citizens of Uniontown to retreat to the mountains. Mountain people were commonly considered isolated, strange, and backward. Hagan later explained to Wright that he and

Kentuck Knob

his wife wished to "partially remove" themselves from urban living. They both loved nature, and Mrs. Hagan especially enjoyed plants, flowers, and landscaping. The site they chose was a knob, or rounded hill, rising from the eastern slopes of Chestnut Ridge about 2,050 feet above sea level, high above the grand horseshoe bend of the Youghiogheny River and the village of Ohiopyle (fig.1).[4]

The name "Kentuck Knob" derives from a part of Stewart township originally called Little Kentucky, as identified on a map of 1832, and later known as the Kentuck district. After the War of Independence, it is said, a pioneer named David Askins set out for the Kentucky country, but was persuaded to settle instead in eastern Fayette County. He laid claim to a vast stretch of land and was amused to call it his Little Kentucky.[5]

The tract that caught Hagan's eye comprised a little more than 79 acres. He asked Herman Keys, a builder, to serve as his agent; Keys bought the property on July 17, 1953, for $9,000 and transferred it the next day to Hagan and his wife for $1. Part of the knoll had been farmed, and the rest had been timbered. The soil was rocky, and the slopes in some places were steep. Donath Peles and his wife, Anna, both Austro-Hungarian immigrants, had bought the property soon after the outbreak of World War I. In selling it, they retained the right to live the rest of their years in the farmhouse by the road—it was three miles from Ohiopyle and six miles from Chalk Hill—and to keep a cow and make use of the outbuildings and garden. Peles, whose surname eventually was Anglicized to Pellish, also dug coal from the slopes across the road, and tapped the sugar maple trees for syrup.[6]

Vista from Kentuck Knob, looking east

THE PATH TO WRIGHT

Architecture properly commences not at the drafting table but with a piece of ground, the wish to build upon it, and above all the desire to build with distinction. All those circumstances converged at Kentuck Knob in the summer of 1953. Oddly enough, a wedding served as the catalyst.

S. Paul Hagan was a tall and handsome lad who attended preparatory school in Windsor, Connecticut, before he entered Princeton University. He planned to write his senior thesis in the department of art and archaeology. Before he turned twenty-one, he became engaged to Bonnie Palmer, who also lived in Uniontown. They set the wedding for August 11 at the Asbury Methodist Church, not far from his parents' home. The best man was to be James Baker, a Princeton student from New

York who had been Paul's roommate. Baker already knew he wanted to be an architect, and indeed he later became one. He arrived in Uniontown a few days before the wedding. On Sunday morning, August 9, Mr. and Mrs. Hagan took Baker and their son to see Fallingwater.[7]

The famous house on Bear Run was commissioned late in 1934 by Edgar J. Kaufmann, president of Kaufmann's Department Store in Pittsburgh. Wright let almost a year slip by before putting pencil to paper. The house was constructed in 1936–1937, and a servants' wing and guest suite were added in 1939. Kaufmann, an energetic man of many enthusiasms, strode into Hagan's office a few years later to ask a large favor. He wanted Hagan to bottle the milk from a mountain dairy cooperative of farmers around Bear Run. Soon he invited Hagan and his wife to Fallingwater. Their son also came to know the house. In his final year at Princeton, he would write that the Kaufmann house "stands as one of Wright's supreme achievements in organic architecture."[8]

The trip to Fallingwater on August 9 so inspired I. N. Hagan that he composed a letter to Wright the same day. "With each subsequent visit," he wrote, "this great house of yours becomes more entrancing to us. For some time now, it has been our fond hope that we might someday confer with you about the construction of a house for us in the mountains. We have now acquired some land and are ready to explore the possibility of building."

Hagan's letter should have caught Wright's attention because of the link to Kaufmann, who had been one of his most generous patrons. Moreover, the possibility of a mountain site that would enhance the drama of his architecture, which in every way emulated the splendors of nature, should have immediately appealed to him. Then, too, Wright had been asserting that culture could no longer thrive in cities; the motor car, he said, gave every American the means to live more independently, and far out in the countryside. Yet he made no effort to respond quickly. Perhaps he was too busy, or perhaps Hagan's approach was too tentative.[9]

"All along," Hagan continued, "we have been firmly persuaded that when the time arrived that we might afford to build, that we might have you commissioned to do the work for us. Contrarywise, we have been equally persuaded that we cannot because of our restricted resources. . . . Mr. Kaufmann contends, however, that such would not be the case. Is there any satisfactory manner in which we might resolve our dilemma? Would it be possible for us to visit with you in Wisconsin?"

Very soon Mr. and Mrs. Hagan visited Bear Run again. Paul Hagan and his bride had flown to Hawaii for their honeymoon, but a few members of the wedding party lingered in Uniontown. One was W. Philip Cotton Jr., of Columbia, Missouri, another classmate from Princeton. Cotton, too, planned to become an architect. He recalls that I. N. Hagan spoke of hiring Deeter and Ritchey, a Pittsburgh firm of architects, to design the mountain house. Cotton went with Hagan and his wife to see Fallingwater, and also to see Kentuck Knob. "I sensed that they very much admired Fallingwater," he said recently. "For about three days I hinted and suggested to them that they hire Wright. Mrs. Hagan just laughed, in a very nice way, every time I would bring the subject up, and I. N. said *nothing*. One evening when we were in the mountains at a restaurant—I can still picture being at the table, the three of us—suddenly I. N. said, 'Let's go see Wright.' Mrs. Hagan turned pale, just simply the shock of it. She had just been jesting, and he had been thinking about this very seriously for two or three days. He called Edgar Kaufmann, and Kaufmann called Wright, and a day or so later we were on our way to Taliesin."[10]

Apart from their visits to Fallingwater, Hagan and his wife knew little about Wright's work or even the location of his home, Taliesin. Hagan had addressed his letter to "Green Springs, Madison, Wisconsin." Cotton drove them west in his family car, a green Chrysler cheerfully complementary to the Cherokee red that Wright favored for his own cars. They encountered Wright as he was walking from his home to Hillside, the complex of buildings where his apprentices occupied a large drafting room. Wright spoke to the Hagans at length and asked about their requirements, interests, and hobbies. They asked for a house with three bedrooms and only two bathrooms. Mrs. Hagan particularly wanted a basement for food storage; she meant to be prepared for winter blizzards. (Although, in nearly thirty years, she recalls, they were snowbound only once.)

The Hagans considered themselves exceedingly fortunate that Wright was so attentive, but in fact he never rejected new work. An architect without the opportunity to build, Wright had learned during lean years, could be little more than a fantasist or theoretician. To win potential clients, he called on a full repertoire of special effects: a stentorian voice, unusual clothing, an aura of invincible self-confidence, and, not least, the ineffable beauty of the buildings and the landscape he had created at Taliesin.[11]

At the end of the day, Wright suggested they see other examples of his work in southern Wisconsin. "Just go and knock on the doors," Cotton recalls him saying, "and the people will welcome you." Hagan reported on their journey when he next wrote Wright from Uniontown, on August 25. They were greatly impressed, he said, by the Johnson Wax Buildings in Racine. They also saw the Herbert Jacobs house (1936–1937) in Madison, the first of the affordable houses Wright built for what he designated "Usonia," or the United States of North America. But they especially admired the Richard Smith house in Jefferson, designed in 1950, and the Unitarian Meeting House (1947–1951) in Shorewood Hills, a suburb of Madison. Notably, both buildings had stone walls and plans based entirely on angles of 60 and 120 degrees. The roof of the Smith house was edged with trellis openings and a pattern of dentils, while the Meeting House had a copper roof with battens that created long streamlines. Wright now had the clues he needed, and Hagan asked him to proceed "with the clear understanding that we cannot under any circumstances spend more than $60,000."[12]

To their great disappointment, the Hagans gradually realized that Wright had no intention of traveling to Pennsylvania to inspect at firsthand their building site. He would rely instead on a topographical survey and a series of photographs that depicted the site and the vistas from it. The exact location of the house, in consequence, became a great problem.

The Hagans visited Taliesin again on September 12, this time with their son and his bride, and by chance it was Paul's twenty-first birthday. Wright graciously staged a dinner celebration and a program of music. Later that month Paul returned to Princeton and changed his thesis topic from the "motor car and its influence on modern art" to an exposition of Wright's work and the concept of an organic architecture. He eventually also considered the work of Le Corbusier, whom Wright detested. Having visited Taliesin, he could write that Wright regarded Le Corbusier as the enemy and referred to other European modernists as the "Bauhaus boys." Paul also described Taliesin as a friendly place surrounded by friendly cows. "It is a rambling house," he wrote, "which clings to its hill and wanders over it as if it were loath to raise itself above the ground at all."[13]

When he wrote to Wright again, on September 28, I. N. explained that the road between Chalk Hill and Ohiopyle was hidden from the southward vistas from below the top of the knoll. To the southeast about four miles, an eminence known as Sugarloaf Knob rose about 2,660 feet above sea level, and to the southwest about five miles, the site of Fort Necessity testified to the fact that long before Fayette County was organized in 1783, its most important historical events had taken place—the incidents of 1754, in which George Washington, then only twenty-two, engaged in the first skirmishes of the final French and Indian War.[14]

"To any but us," Hagan wrote, "the top of the knoll probably presents a pretty discouraging picture. The ground is literally covered with stones . . . in such abundance that we could use them easily for the construction of a road and, or, stone walls. All of this makes us wonder whether we might not be able to unearth a sufficient supply of stones for building purposes right on the property."

Hagan had visited Fallingwater again, because Kaufmann offered him stones from the quarry just west of the house. But the cost of transporting them, he wrote, made it more economical to locate stone on his own property. The budget, he repeated, was not to exceed $60,000, including all incidentals. Hagan knew from Kaufmann that Wright could be prodigal. Wright circled the budget and the reference to stone walls, but he drew a line through Hagan's mention of the top of the knoll. The highest point of any site, he believed, should be left free.[15]

Later that fall, Hagan and his wife traveled to New York and toured the Usonian house built on the future site of the Guggenheim Museum to accompany "Sixty Years of Living Architecture," a major exhibition of Wright's work. They found the house enrapturing, Hagan wrote. Many of the features would soon appear in the plans for Kentuck: a living room with a wall of glass at one side and with clerestory windows, bookshelves, and a built-in seat at the other; French doors to a terrace sheltered by a cantilevered roof perforated with trellis openings; a dining alcove close by the kitchen, or workspace, and a narrow gallery, or corridor, to the relatively small bedrooms.

At Taliesin it was time for the annual migration to Wright's desert camp near Phoenix, Arizona. Eugene Masselink, a senior apprentice who specialized in graphic design but also served as Wright's secretary, wrote Hagan on November 7 that his house would be designed "shortly after we are back at work at Taliesin West." Wright himself sent a brief note on December 17: "You are 'in work.'" By then, however, the Hagans were having second thoughts. They were considering a flat roof and board-and-batten walls instead of stone. "Perhaps all this would have been better left unsaid," Hagan wrote at the end of 1953, "for we realize that your judgment is infinitely superior to our own."

Wright had the design firmly in mind; the walls would be of stone and the copper roof would not be flat. The Hagans received a package from Taliesin West on February 13, and at last they saw the preliminary sketches for their house on Kentuck Knob.

PLANS AND REVISIONS

The sketches delighted Mr. and Mrs. Hagan (figs. 2–4). They had been prepared, evidently, by John H. Howe, the chief drafts-man, who joined the Taliesin Fellowship at its inception in the fall of 1932 and served for many years as a loyal pencil in the master's hand.[16]

First among the sketches was the plan. It showed a grav-eled entrance court, framed as if by pincers, and a living room that established a dominant axis from which the bedrooms veered at an obtuse angle. Plans of this kind, Wright wrote in *The Natural House,* were shaped "like polliwogs." The living room and kitchen constituted the head or body, and the bed-rooms formed the tail. In any event, the plan for Kentuck looked

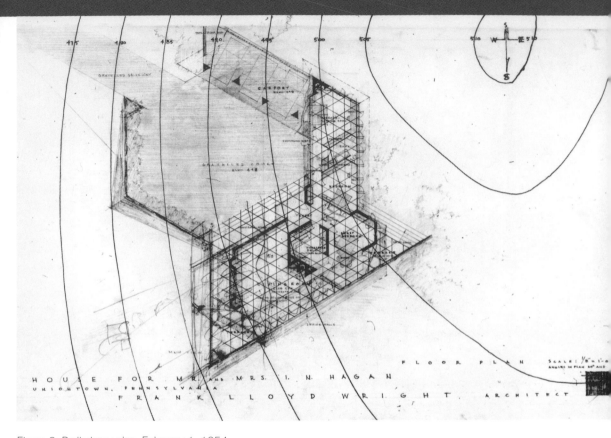

Figure 2. Preliminary plan, February 1, 1954

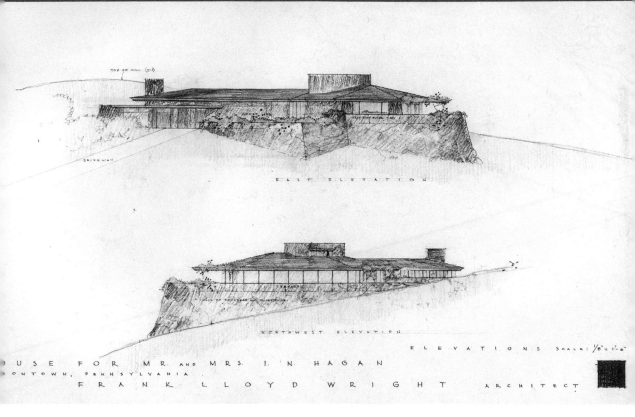

EAST ELEVATION

NORTHWEST ELEVATION

ELEVATIONS SCALE: 1/8"=1'-0"

HOUSE FOR MR. AND MRS. I. N. HAGAN
KENTOWN, PENNSYLVANIA.
FRANK LLOYD WRIGHT ARCHITECT

Figure 3. Elevation sketches, February 1, 1954

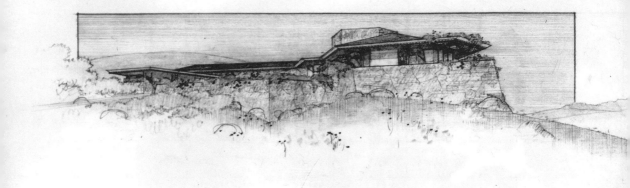

VIEW FROM EAST

HOUSE FOR MR. AND MRS. I. N. HAGAN
UNIONTOWN, PENNSYLVANIA
FRANK LLOYD WRIGHT ARCHITECT

Figure 4. Perspective, February 1, 1954

amazingly alive. It also showed how the masonry bearing walls and piers would be condensed and dispersed to free the perimeter of the house for long reaches of windows and glass doors. On a second sheet, two elevation drawings depicted the house nestled somewhat below the crown of the hill. Finally, a perspective view presented Kentuck rising nobly from the slopes.[17]

But the vitality of the sketches could not conceal their surprising carelessness. Wright's studio was overwhelmed with work. Drawings were under way for the Price Tower, in Bartlesville, Oklahoma, the only skyscraper to be built from Wright's plans, and for the Beth Sholom Synagogue, in Elkins Park, north of Philadelphia. Continual changes in the plans for the Guggenheim Museum demanded great effort, and other houses were being designed. With so much to do, Wright relied on the senior apprentices and on various procedures and details that had become standard. He lacked the time and the stamina to give his full attention to every project.[18]

The volume of work also burdened Howe. Given time, he was an accomplished and meticulous draftsman; but the sketches for Kentuck abounded with evidence of haste. They misrepresented the contours of the knoll, gave elevations above sea level more than 1,500 feet in error and even misoriented the house to the north. (Later, the compass points were erased and reversed, but still not shown accurately.) The plan positioned the window wall of the living room only two feet from the terrace parapet. Four different geometric figures were generated by the complicated grid, and finally the unit for construction proved to be a difficult fractional dimension.

As they studied the sketches, Hagan and his wife rightly judged the body of the "polliwog" to be too small and stubby. He wanted a larger living room, and she wanted a bigger kitchen. They also found the dining arrangement unsatisfactory; five chairs were to be crowded around a small hexagonal table with a tiny triangular extension. They could not envision where the house was to be sited. Hagan had put the question to Wright much earlier, and it would go unanswered for several months to come. ("We still can't clearly determine the location you have proposed," he wrote on April 14, and he reported on May 10 that after staking out the site according to the plan, "we have discovered that this makes for a seemingly impossible solution for a satisfactory driveway.")[19]

The plan sketch had been prepared in Wright's standard way, with the principal front of the house tilted at thirty degrees. "Surveyors do not seem to have learned that the south is the comforter of life, the south side of the house the 'living' side," Wright remarked in *The Natu-*

ral House. "Ordinarily the house should be set 30–60 to the south, well back on its site so that every room in the house might have sunlight some time in the day. . . . The sun is the great luminary of all life." His procedure first identified the horizontal of the T-square on the drafting board with east and west on a topographical map. By placing a thirty-sixty degree triangle on the T-square with the smaller angle at the lower left, he aligned the principal face of the house with the hypotenuse. This set the axis of orientation at 150 degrees on the compass, or seven and a half degrees east of south-southeast. It was how he had sketched the plan for Fallingwater.[20]

The same procedure appeared in an undated "Supplementary Plot Plan" for Kentuck, although the compass points had been rotated slightly to the left. But when the plan was revised on March 15—no doubt because Hagan had written that he and his wife would soon visit Taliesin West—it oriented the house slightly to the south of south-southeast (fig. 5). And that eventually was the way it was built. Such was the confusion, however, that the first set of working drawings, prepared in April, reverted to the usual 150-degree axis of orientation, some fifteen degrees eastward. After all that, Mrs. Hagan recalls the house being moved westward; the final rotation of the house more to the south had indeed shifted the salient angle of the living room to the west.

None of the problems with the drawings could diminish Wright's imaginative conception of the floor plan. It, too, sprang from the thirty-sixty triangle. The great virtues of the "one-two triangle," as Wright called it, inhered in the vigor of its acute angles and in the elegant simplicity of the fact that its shortest side measured exactly half the length of the longest, the hypotenuse. Thus, two thirty-sixty triangles could compose an equilateral triangle of sixty-degree angles. Two con-joined equilateral triangles, in turn, formed angles of 120 degrees. Wright began to experiment with 120-degree angles in his "Honey-comb" house (1936–1937) in Palo Alto, California. "I am convinced," he wrote, "that a cross-section of honeycomb has more fertility and flexibility where human movement is concerned than the square."[21]

Hence the key to Wright's conception of Kentuck appeared in a brief legend on the plan sketch: "Angles in plan 60° and 120°." The acute angles would thrust the house into the landscape, while the obtuse angles would let it embrace the hill and at the same time open the interior space in unexpected ways. The angular plan would also respond to the distant mountain landscape; Wright had noted in the Southwest that "mountain ranges are all 60–30 triangles unless your eye is arrested by an effect produced by one that is equilateral. A

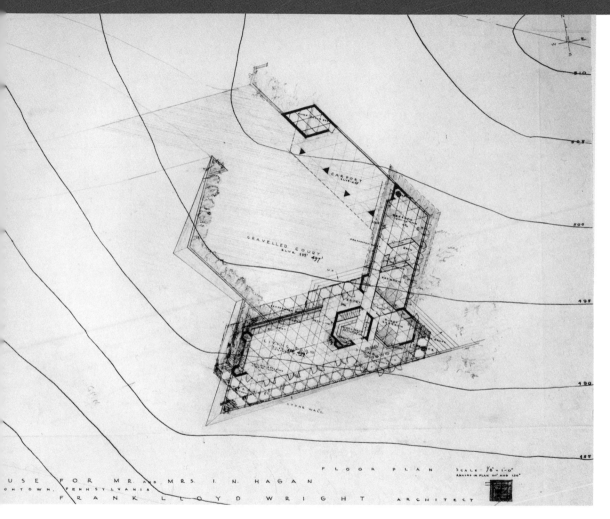

Figure 5. Revised plan, March 15, 1954

cross-section of the talus [rock debris] at the base of the mountains is the hypotenuse of a 30–60 triangle."[22]

Wright discerned in nature a variety of underlying geometric patterns. Even stone formations, he thought, were essentially geometric and could therefore offer the architect inspiring "marvels of beauty." He believed architecture to be a profoundly geometric and abstract art, indeed more abstract than music. But his geometric sense of nature and architecture could not easily account for the difficult plan grid of Kentuck. Although his standard grid of sixty-degree and 120-degree angles also derived from only three pairs of crisscrossed equidistant parallel lines, its pattern presented a clear mosaic of equilateral triangles (fig. 6). Because every side of every triangle measured the same length, there could be no doubt about the unit, or module, of construction. Moreover, he usually gave the unit an ordinary or whole-number dimension, such as four feet. Sometimes he omitted the horizontal lines to create instead a mosaic of equilateral parallelograms, commonly called a "diamond" pattern. By comparison with either grid, the pattern for Kentuck, as illustrated explicitly in the working drawings, looked like a child's game of pick-up-sticks (fig. 7).[23]

The pattern comprised four small triangles, a central hexagon, and two overlapped equilateral parallelograms. When extended, it also

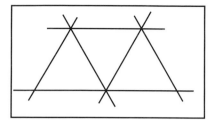

Figure 6.
Wright's typical angled plan-grid

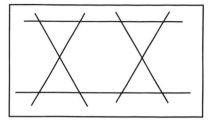

Figure 7.
Plan-grid for Kentuck

generated a hexagram, or six-pointed star (fig. 8). Although the hexagram appeared of little relevance to the floor plan, any of the other figures seemed eligible to serve as the unit. The critical unit dimension would determine the window and door openings, the walls and partitions, and even the length of the dining table.

Howe had typically sketched the plan without dimensions but at a scale of one-eighth of an inch to one foot. In drawing the plan to scale, he mistakenly gave whole-number dimensions to the interior perpen-

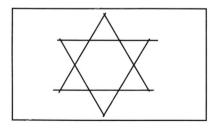

Figure 8. Kentuck plan-grid extended

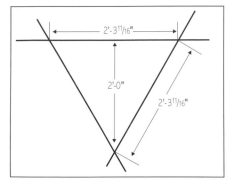

Figure 9. Dimensioned triangle from plan grid

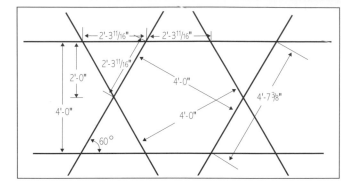

Figure 10. Unit dimensions of Kentuck plan

diculars of each geometric figure: two feet from the apex of each small triangle to the opposite side, four feet between the opposite sides of the hexagon and—as someone, perhaps Wright, later wrote on the sketch—eight feet between the apexes of the parallelogram, or rhombus.

All the geometric figures could be constructed from copies of the small triangle, and only one, again the triangle, could tesselate, or form a mosaic from, the entire plan. Given a perpendicular dimension of 2 feet, the sides of each triangle measured 2' 3$^{11}/_{16}$": the half-unit (fig. 9). The full unit thus equaled two sides of triangles and measured 4' 7$^{3}/_{8}$" (fig. 10).[24]

A well-conceived unit system, Wright said, could "keep all to scale, ensure consistent proportion throughout the edifice, large or small, which thus became—like tapestry—a consistent fabric woven of interdependent, related units, however various." Such a system was also intended to simplify the plan and facilitate construction. Wright saw great beauty in the unit system, which he preferred to expose by scoring the concrete floors with all the unit lines. But he must not have noticed the egregious dimension of the unit for Kentuck, and the undimensioned working drawings, with a unit of 4' 7³/₈" must have astounded Herman Keys, the builder.[25]

Wright made his first revisions directly on the plan sketch. To lengthen the living room, he simply added two units. The room grew slightly longer in the March 15 plan, and longer still in the working drawings (fig. 11). At the same time, Wright narrowed the room by moving the stationary windows and the French doors much farther away from the terrace parapet. He also changed the small west terrace into a large planting box, and adroitly enlarged the dining alcove by enclosing the east end of the south terrace.

Although the March 15 plan improved the configuration of the steps to the entry, it still sacrificed a good part of the kitchen for steps to the basement. Eventually the basement stair was shifted into the "tail" of the house, clearly a victory for Mrs. Hagan. But in other matters Wright proved not so accommodating. The Hagans asked for

Thermopane, an insulating glass from the Libbey Owens Ford Company with double panes separated by sealed and dehydrated air. They believed the extra cost could be recovered over the years by savings in heating oil. Wright nevertheless insisted on using polished plate glass. He also balked when Hagan asked him to send "Davy" Davison to oversee the construction of the house.

Allen L. Davison was a senior apprentice who answered only to Wright. He had spoken with the Hagans on their first visit to Taliesin. His interest in their project—he came from a suburb of Pittsburgh—may have been the reason he was assigned to the working drawings. Fellow apprentices remember Davison for his imaginative nighttime renderings of some of Wright's larger projects. They also recall that he was clumsy in preparing working drawings, which helps to account for the inconsistencies and awkward details in those for Kentuck. Davison nonetheless befriended the Hagans and contrived to visit their building site informally whenever he traveled back to Pittsburgh.[26]

(In his enthusiasm for Wright's services, Hagan asked him to redesign a small office building for the ice cream company. The footings for a two-story building were already in place, but Hagan had been disappointed by various sketches submitted by a Uniontown architect. The preliminary sketches from Taliesin West arrived on April 13.

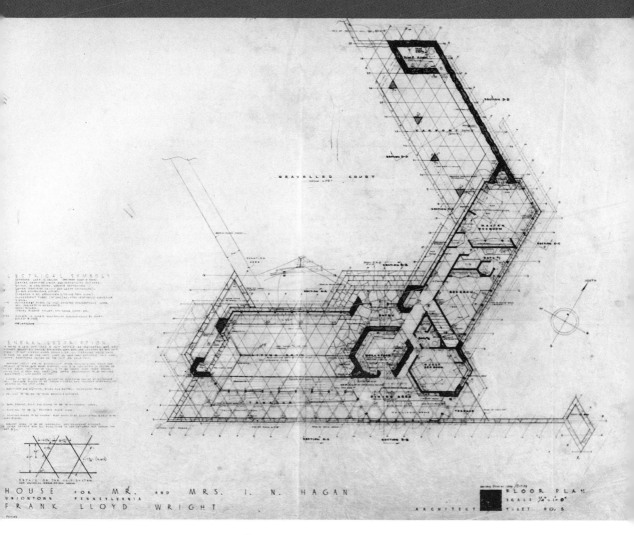

Figure 11. Working drawing of Kentuck plan, with unit diagram (lower left)

They envisioned a three-story building with an apartment on the top floor. Hagan responded that he was "thoroughly fascinated" and astonished at how quickly the drawings had been produced. The design in fact was a potboiler. Wright sent a bill later that month for $2,500. Hagan paid him promptly but soon postponed the project. Eventually it was abandoned.)[27]

Wright had already charged $3,000 for the preliminary sketches of Kentuck, 5 percent of the construction budget. He sent another bill, for $3,750, at the end of April, when five sets of blueprints and specifications were mailed to Uniontown. This time, he unilaterally raised the construction budget to $75,000. "We were considerably taken aback," Hagan wrote on May 10. "We determined, from the outset, that we could not conceivably spend more than $60,000 on this venture." Two weeks later, Herman Keys told him it could take $35,000 just to build the house up to floor level; the entire project, Keys estimated, would cost $124,000. Hagan wrote Wright that he and his wife were left "quite depressed about the whole affair."

After the house was complete, Hagan calculated his expenses at $82,329 for construction, $12,106 for furnishings and $1,622 for landscaping: a total of $96,057. He told Wright that "the eventual cost was far in excess of our anticipation." Hagan was not making allowance, however, for all the changes and improvements—the substantial enlargement of the living room, a slight extension of the master bedroom, a major extension of the storage room, the change from mahogany to tidewater red cypress for all the woodwork, the paving of the entire floor with flagstones, and the cost of first-class furnishings. In light of all those items, the budget was kept very well under control. Far more important, and in spite of every difficulty, the house achieved all that Wright imagined. It truly upheld "the honor of the work."[28]

Surely much of the credit belonged to Herman Keys and the various tradesmen. Keys was seventy-three when he began to prepare the building-site; the only time Wright visited Kentuck Knob, so far as Mr. and Mrs. Hagan knew, he referred to Keys as "the old man," although he himself was fourteen years older. Keys was best known in Uniontown for having built the State Theater on Main Street, a handsome structure distinguished by three large arches in polychromed terra cotta. When he went with Hagan to see Fallingwater, however, Keys worried whether he would have the ability to construct a house designed by Wright. "But he launched into it," Hagan once said, "and did it perfectly. He was a great craftsman and a perfectionist."[29]

Keys poured concrete retaining walls to hold the compacted dirt fill and broken stone that formed the podium below the floor. Down the slopes, five or six men split boulders with sledgehammers and wedges, stone picks and jackhammers. They trucked the stones to the entrance court. Jesse Wilson, a master mason from Markleysburg, at the southeast corner of the county, worked with one of his sons, Jesse J. Wilson, in hammer dressing the stones into roughly rectangular shape. They left the faces untouched. Wilson laid a sample wall for approval, and Davison stressed the importance of attending to the horizontal character of the house. The parts were to belong to the whole (fig. 12). Some stones would project several inches beyond the wall-face; in the parlance of Taliesin, these were the "stickouts," intended to give the walls a natural and lively syncopated rhythm. The walls were to be laid in random ranges—layers—somewhat like those of Fallingwater, where Wilson found the sandstone to have less warmth and color.[30]

The colors throughout Kentuck would be more limited than at Fallingwater but also subtler, and greatly enriched by the surfaces in tidewater red cypress, a wood of such appeal to Wright that he is still remembered in the lumber trade for using so much of it. "He loved cypress, called it the 'wood eternal.' But he had a special affection for swamp cypress, calling it 'more eternal,'" Edgar Tafel, one of the origi-

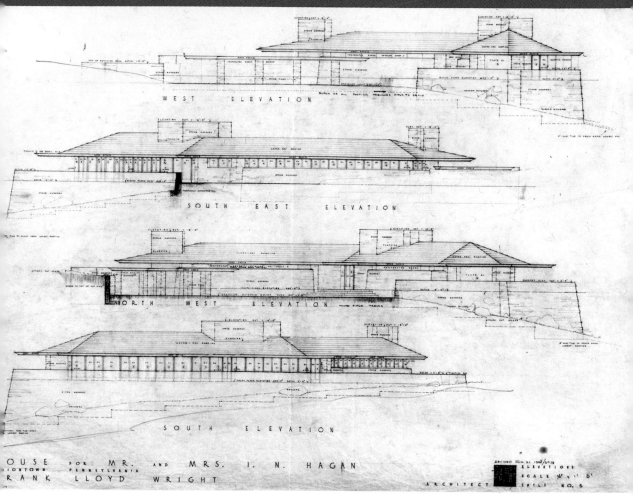

WEST ELEVATION

SOUTH EAST ELEVATION

NORTH WEST ELEVATION

SOUTH ELEVATION

OUSE FOR MR. AND MRS. I. N. HAGAN
IONTOWN PENNSYLVANIA

RANK LLOYD WRIGHT

ARCHITECT

ELEVATIONS
SCALE ¼" = 1' 8"
SHEET NO. 5

Figure 12. Working drawing of elevations

nal Taliesin apprentices, recalled. Known commonly as bald cypress, because the tree sheds its hemlock-like leaves in the fall, the wood indeed resists rotting. Wright often asserted, contrary to fact, that wood best preserved itself. At the same time, paradoxically, he believed in change and defined decay as "another form of growth." Someone at Taliesin knew better, because the specifications for Kentuck called for a durable finish. Hagan found it too glossy and inquired how the exterior cypress should be treated. "Nothing but the weather," Wright responded. Fortunately, the finish was finally applied, and it protected the wood against discoloring and turning black.[31]

Clarence S. Coughenour, the millwork foreman at the Charles F. Eggers Lumber Company in Uniontown, undertook all the woodwork. Eggers recalls that a lumber supplier in Pittsburgh assembled the wood from various sources and sent to Uniontown "almost a full car load of clear, all-heart tidewater red cypress." Hagan recalled of Coughenour, who was sixty-nine when he began work on Kentuck, that "to him it was a challenge. . . . He was a real artist, and he was very helpful."[32]

From the first, Wright planned to roof the house in sheet copper. He called copper the king of sheet metals. "Its verdigris," he wrote, "is always a great beauty in connection with stone or brick or wood." The roof of Kentuck was pitched at an angle of only twenty degrees, and the copper was stepped over horizontal battens to shape a series of swift streamlines. Henry J. Cooper, a Uniontown contractor, installed the roof with copper (from the Revere Copper and Brass Plant in Rome, New York).[33]

But the drawings for the underlying roof structure had proved an embarrassment. "Herman remains adamant in his contention that the roof is fragile and improperly supported," Hagan warned Davison as early as August 1954. The drawings showed a very large and long steel beam at the living-room ridge, several lesser steel members (two of which failed to bear directly on any support), and a series of nine wood struts at the south wall. "With the enormous wind pressure we are apt to encounter on the mountain top together with the massive download of the roof," Hagan wrote, "there inevitably will be movement of the studs."

Wright finally visited the building site. He arrived with Edgar Kaufmann jr., who had been a Taliesin apprentice when his father commissioned the house on Bear Run. Mrs. Hagan had been discouraged by the ragged building site and was excited to hear Wright remark, "Junior, this is marvelous!" But when Wright reviewed the blueprints with Herman Keys, he was forced to agree that the living room was going to lack sufficient wracking strength. He returned to Taliesin and gathered the apprentices. He told them he had just been corrected by a mountain contractor in Pennsylvania. "He was furious," Curtis Besinger recalls. The roof framing had to be redesigned and the wood supports were reconfigured to conceal steel stanchions.[34]

The Hagans soon realized that beyond all the amenities that would be finished in cypress—the long seat at the north wall of the living room, the cabinets, the bookshelves, the dining table, sideboard, and so on—they would need freestanding pieces such as chairs and tables. Ideally, for Wright, the architectural grammar of a building would infuse every piece of furniture, and every detail would testify to the same severe discipline of design. During his long career he had conceived some majestically architectonic pieces, but too many of the chairs, as he readily confessed, were not at all comfortable. And by the time of Kentuck he was much too busy, and probably too old, to invent special pieces of furniture for every new commission. So when Hagan asked for a hassock and some low tables for the living room, Wright merely suggested pieces he had sketched for the Heritage Henredon collection. *House Beautiful* had just introduced a "Taliesin Ensemble" of commercial furniture, fabrics, rugs, paints, and even wallpaper "for the general homemaker, rather than for special clients." One line, developed from drawings by Curtis Besinger, offered triangular tables and stools that could be grouped into hexagons; it might have seemed eligible for the house on Kentuck Knob.[35]

Hagan and his wife, however, did not consider themselves general homemakers. From reading *An Autobiography,* Hagan had concluded that Wright was vastly interested in "gracious living." He himself liked fine cars, fine cameras, fine fishing gear, and a style of life distinctly elevated above that of most residents of Uniontown. The same issue of *House Beautiful* carried an advertisement by the Georg Jensen showroom in New York for handmade furniture designed in Denmark by Hans J. Wegner, who liked to say that "a chair is not finished until someone sits in it." With advice from Edgar Kaufmann jr., who had directed the industrial design department at the Museum of Modern Art, and with Paul Mayen, a friend of Kaufmann's and an interior designer entitled to professional discounts, the Hagans visited the Jensen shop and bought some Wegner chairs. For the cushions of the long built-in seat they chose a fabric designed by Jack Lenor Larsen, who had opened a New York studio in 1951. And from Kaufmann's Department Store in Pittsburgh they ordered all the Moroccan rugs for the house.[36]

But the furnishings that would sound the dominant chord came from the American woodworker George Nakashima. By chance,

Kaufmann had just written in *Art in America* of the "direct poetry and vigor" of Nakashima's furniture and praised his studio in New Hope, Pennsylvania, as "a clear spring of design enterprise." Trained as an architect, Nakashima built his own showroom, which Kaufmann illustrated. Mr. and Mrs. Hagan expressed an interest, and Kaufmann urged them to drive to New Hope, which they did. In March 1956 they ordered their first pieces, a long coffee table for the built-in seat of the living room and a special cabinet, seven feet long, for the entry. The next month they ordered a cushion chair, a stool, an ottoman, and six grass-seated chairs for the dining table. By the time the house was finished, they had ordered fifteen pieces, nearly all in walnut.[37]

Nakashima, a man of independent spirit, possessed a rare feel for wood and the idiosyncratic markings of solid planks, which he excelled at revealing. Ironically, an angular house of Wright's caused him to give up architecture for woodworking; he saw the Honeycomb house in construction. "I found the structure and the bones of the building somehow inadequate," he wrote much later, "and the workmanship shoddy. I felt that I must find a new vocation." Not surprisingly, he was not eager to take special orders for a house designed by Wright, replete with sixty-degree and 120-degree angles. Nakashima, unlike Wright, scorned veneers as "fake." And contrary to the strict geometric discipline of Wright's work, he liked the free edge of a board "debarked but otherwise left with a natural edge." He nevertheless accommodated the Hagans, adopted a few sixty-degree angles to make certain pieces accord with the floor-plan, and later visited their house.[38]

George Nakashima's furniture showroom, 1954
(Ezra Stoller © ESTO)

It took until the summer of 1956 to complete the house. The Hagans moved in to the almost completed house on July 29, to celebrate their twenty-sixth wedding anniversary. More than a year later, Hagan sent Wright the final payment of his fee, which represented 10 percent of the total costs. "With the actual construction behind us," he wrote, "we now tend to look upon the house as a great climax in our lives. To live in it is a privilege. As a work of art it is a continuing revelation."

THE HOUSE COMPLETE

The lane to Kentuck is less than half a mile long. Rising through a forest of mostly deciduous trees, it conveys very quickly the sense of a private and tranquil place. The house comes into view slowly and looks as if it is an outcropping from the hill. During the warmer months, it is virtually hidden as the lane draws closer. Finally, the lane reaches a copper lamp standard designed after the house was finished. Both the lamp and the stone planter are constituted from angles that announce the character of the house itself, and at the opposite side, the roof of the storage room is acutely angled and cantilevered almost six feet past its support. Like a forest clearing, the court is suffused with serenity and wonder. It possesses the spirit Wright so admired in the traditional architecture of Japan.

Lane to the house

View from the lane

Approach to entrance court

Lamp at entrance court

Entrance court, looking east

Carports and bedroom wing, looking east

Many features of the house express the quiet poetry of the horizontal: the entry steps, the clerestory, the streamlines of the copper roof, the precise alignment of the long, flat roof over the carports with the coping stones of the gallery. In the absence of a human figure, the scale remains elusive and even deceptive. Clues to the intimacy of the house reside in certain dimensions. Each step to the entry, for instance, rises only about four inches. The ceiling of the carports stands six feet, four inches, high, and each face of the triangular stone piers measures only a half-unit wide.

Storage room, looking north

Originally, the carports were to end at a triangular utility room with a well-water pump. Through several revisions of the plan, the room continued to grow across the graveled court. It came to serve Mrs. Hagan as a studio for her painting. When her husband demolished an old barn at the other side of the Chalk Hill-Ohiopyle road, she used the weathered boards to panel the storage-room walls.

Overview, looking south

Top of the knoll, looking east

From behind the carports and storage room, a winter vantage presents the angular shape of the house and shows how it backs into the knoll. "Hill and house," Wright wrote of Taliesin, "should live together each the happier for the other." The crown of the hill left free can flourish as a copse, a special place of even further retreat.[39]

At the other side of the court and down the slope, the house presents a much different face. Now the formative principles of Wright's architecture become more evident. The living space is lifted upon a high podium, and the cantilevered roof appears borne aloft by only two stone piers. A broad rift between the roof and the mass of ma-

Living room and terrace, looking southeast

sonry below it creates the sense of an open-air pavilion in the forest, a refuge that kindles the spirit with the feeling of expansive freedom.

The podium slopes sharply inward, in sympathy with the hill, and the structure grows lighter as it rises, an effect Wright described earlier as "the sense of physical weight dissolved in space." From a different perspective, the house looks still more dramatic. The perforated roof forms a colossal horizontal trellis of hexagonal openings as it sails askew from the masonry prow, which surges nearly eighteen

Terrace prow, looking northeast

feet into the air. Herman Keys was inspired to call the house the "Queen Mary."[40]

The axis of the roof in fact diverges sixty degrees from that of the prow. This extraordinary disjunction makes clear that the roof will not fit like the lid on a box, and Kentuck will overcome all the confining conditions of a conventional dwelling. Structural equilibrium is necessary for any building, but here it becomes more vital and occult.

"Obvious symmetry," Wright remarked, "usually closes the epi-
sode before it begins."[41]

In writing about Taliesin,
which he began to build in 1911,
Wright said his sense of architecture by then had become "some-
thing in league with the stones

South face

of the field." Kentuck joins the ground from which its stones were
extracted. The boulders left unsplit were so cunningly placed that
when Jesse Wilson arrived at the site, he assumed they had always
been there.[42]

From points farther along the garden path the house again appears serene. Its long horizontals bring to mind those of the great prairie houses Wright conceived half a century earlier, but now they sug-
gest an abstraction of the sedimentary rock-structure pattern of Stewart
township. Rock masses sculpted by wind and water, Wright had noted,
"take on the streamlines characteristic of the sweeping forces that
change them."[43]

The parapet keeps company with the cantilevered roof, and both

South face, looking northwest

assert the horizontal—"the true earth-line of human life," Wright wrote, "indicative of freedom. Always." And because the middle zone is transformed from a wall into a light screen of windows and glass doors, Kentuck overcomes the traditional agent of confinement.[44]

The house reaches higher ground at the east, where the south face ends with a great stone planter shaped like a parallelogram. The scale quickly changes to one of gentle domesticity. Glass doors open to a terrace planned originally as a grassy lawn. The Hagans instead paved it with flagstones and added a triangular pool and rock garden. The first few windows onto the terrace belong to the guest room. The other bedrooms and the bathroom between them are lighted by the long series of windows in the tail of the house, which recedes into the hilltop.

At close range, the characteristic angled details at the cornice accentuate the sheltering roof. Now the one-two triangle serves to set the fascia boards at a thirty-degree angle, and the subfascia boards are notched with continuous two-inch dentils to create a long "dotted line," as Wright envisioned it, again to ornament the horizontal.[45]

The entrance to Kentuck, at the court, is sheltered but not concealed. It conveniently connects to the carports by a short walk. The low risers and deep treads, so swift to the eye, paradoxically slow the

Garden terrace, looking west

Bedroom wing, looking north

Entrance, looking southwest

approach and invite a more leisurely appreciation of the stone masonry and its muted colors: golden tan, gray, brown, violet, and red. At
the clerestory, which forms an openwork light screen of perforated
cypress boards, each panel measures one unit long. Almost all the
cutouts play with thirty- and sixty-degree angles, and because every
other panel is reversed, the pattern rises and falls like a mountain
ridge. The wall thus dissolves as it meets the soffits, or undersides, of
the roof, which are also paneled in cypress.[46]

Entry, looking northeast

In place of a single door and an abrupt division of indoors from out, the entrance takes the form of a folding screen in four panels, all transparent. The side lights, like those of many windows at Fallingwater, sink directly into the stonework, and the wall thus seems to change effortlessly from a massive and opaque material to one almost invisible. The kitchen wall stands only six feet away, but it turns the corner obliquely to shape a vista of more than fifty feet across the living room. By contrast, the gallery to the bedrooms demands a backward turn of 120 degrees—to discourage intrusion of the more private quarters.

Sandstone and cypress and glass come together in a simple harmony at the entry and throughout the house; the entire floor, except in the kitchen, is paved with flagstone. The Hagans asked for ceilings a little higher than usual with Wright, because their son stood six feet two inches tall. In rising to six feet seven inches, the entry ceiling nevertheless reaches only one inch above the sum of six vertical units, each being defined by the combined width of a board and a batten, or thirteen inches.

Entry, looking west

The battens are recessed, in a reversal of ordinary construction, and secured to a plywood core. Milled with alternate lapped and tongue-in-groove joints, they are intended to hold the boards and leave untouched the broad pattern of the grain. Although the working drawings called for screws in the battens only, countersunk finish nails were used at Kentuck. The paneling is nonetheless elegant, and it revels in the beauty of cypress as it reiterates the horizontal.[47]

By continuing into the living room, the entry ceiling changes into the soffit of a broad deck above the built-in seat. Small light boxes shaped as equilateral triangles punctuate the long plane. The front edges of the bookshelves are visually strengthened with fascias as wide as the exposed surfaces of the battens; they reinforce the horizontal as the ceiling rises into the slope of the roof and reaches eleven feet high. "One of the advantages of the sloping roof," Wright wrote, "is that it gives you a sense of spaciousness inside, a sense of overhead uplift which I often feel to be very good."[48]

As the deck engirds the room, the light boxes illuminate the ceiling above it. The cypress can flower in full glory. Wright had saluted "the beauty of wood as silken-texture or satin-surfaces upon which nature has marked the lines of its character in exquisite drawing and color," and he considered wood to be the most humanly intimate of all materials. He had seen wood ceilings in the traditional houses of Japan; of all civilized nations, he said, the Japanese understood wood best.[49]

The clerestory panels form a delicate frieze of glass to manifest what Wright called the *abstract pattern of structure itself.* At the op-

Living room, north side

posite side of the room, the light screen is composed of stationary windows and French doors opening to the south terrace. The roof projects more than nine feet past the glass to embrace the terrace as an integral part of the house. Hexagonal trellis openings help ventilate the room and can relieve outdoor wind loads; they also enliven the floor by casting sun splashes, an abstraction of forest light. From vari-

Living room, looking northwest

ous points in the living room, the broad plane of the soffits propels the space toward the terrace. At the far end of the room a pane of plate glass four feet tall and more than eight wide opens a vista into the forest. An indoor garden extends into an outdoor planter to encourage the illusion of no glass at all.[50]

A house should be conceived organically, Wright said, as "lived-in space playing with light," and, in any house, "*shelter* should be the essential look." The living room of Kentuck greatly benefits from the privacy and beauty of the mountain site.

Living room, south side

There are no curtains or drapes anywhere in the house. Nor is any room disturbed by visible appurtenances for heating or air-conditioning. Wright thought air-conditioning was "a dangerous circumstance." Instead, he recommended "thorough protection overhead and the rest of the building as open to the breezes as it possibly can be made." Heat comes from a maze of pipes coiled on a bed of broken stone below the floor. Forced hot water warms the floor so well that windows can be left slightly open even in winter.[51]

Wright intended to finish the floor in smooth concrete integrally colored red and scored with every unit line. Flagstones were to be used only at the entry and around the fireplace. Hagan objected to the unit lines, which he thought would make a "thoroughly unsightly ar-

Terrace prow, looking southwest

Terrace, looking west

rangement"; he drew a comparison to the concrete floors of hog barns, commonly scored with crisscrossed grooves to give the animals better footing on smooth and often slippery surfaces. He conceded, however, that Herman Keys considered the "hog rods" vital to the plan. As a builder faced with a most peculiar unit dimension canted at a sixty-degree angle, Keys better understood Wright's purpose in expressing the geometry of the floor plan. Hagan pondered the issue for more

Stationary window, looking west

than a year before he proposed to pave the entire floor with "natural stone." Wright accepted the change, and again Kentuck echoed Fallingwater.[52]

When the masonry walls were still in construction, Hagan chanced upon a stone with an unusual hollow. He asked Wilson to incorporate it into the fireplace hood. There, above the hob, it serves as a cup to hold sticks of tinder. Because the cantilevered stones rely on hidden steel angles and a diagonal tie to the kitchen wall, the fireplace hood can be faulted as a structural anomaly. Yet the stonework and the turns

Living room, looking northeast

that so graciously inflect the living-room space toward both the dining area and the entry perfectly express the character of the house.[53]

The dining alcove appropriates part of the terrace and changes the trellis openings into small skylights. It captures more daylight than any other room. Like the reading alcove at Fallingwater, the dining space also plays upon ambiguities of indoors and out. The ceiling con-

Dining alcove, looking east

tinues at the height of the living-room deck, and the lines of the board-and-batten paneling shift to give the space more definition.

As an integral feature, the dining table extends directly from the sideboard. Its front edges, like those of the open bookshelves, are widened to match the battens. Each section of the table measures one unit, and the cypress veneer is finished to a high gloss. The table stands

(Left) Dining alcove, looking west

(Below) Passage to guest room, looking northeast

conveniently near the kitchen and also close to a very narrow passage to the guest room.[54]

As though the keep of some tiny castle, the kitchen rises from the center of the house in a hollow shaft of stone. Wright had written earlier of "a new thought concerning a kitchen—taking it away from the outside walls and letting it run up into overhead space with the chimney." The kitchen thus seeks light from above. (The domed skylight in fact admitted so much sunlight and heat that an aluminum sun

Kitchen, looking southwest

Kitchen, looking southeast

screen had to be installed. Even so, the ceiling reaches about fourteen and a half feet high.) In plan, the kitchen is an irregular hexagon cut in two by an angled passage from the dining space all the way to the master bedroom. Each opening is spanned by a single stone lintel.[55]

Apart from the wealth of cabinets, nearly every detail of the kitchen represents a change by Mrs. Hagan. For the floor, she chose cork in place of red rubber tiles. Rather than finishing the counters and backsplashes in red Micarta, a plastic, she used stainless steel specially fabricated and continuous with a single steel sink. She chose different ranges, a different oven, and a different dishwasher. The one specified item she accepted was an exhaust fan near the range. In effect, Mrs. Hagan eliminated the color red from the kitchen, just as the paving of the concrete floor eliminated red from all the other rooms. Red was Wright's favorite color, but he made no objection, because none of the changes could compromise the structure and form of the space.[56]

The bedrooms differ in size and plan, but all have ceilings, walls, decks, bookshelves, tables, cabinets, and wardrobes finished in tidewater red cypress. The light levels are low, in part because of the dark wood, and although all the ceilings reach eleven feet high, the rooms can seem close and burrow-like. Twin beds help to reduce the scale of the furniture. The guest room is configured as a hexagon, and two of the windows can open to make a corner vanish, again a detail like one at Fallingwater. The bathroom follows an irregular plan and has two doors, one convenient to the kitchen and entry.[57]

Guest room

Guest room, corner windows

Gallery, looking toward master bedroom

A wide door from the gallery opens to the basement stair. Mrs. Hagan wanted the basement extended under the living room, but Wright refused to provide more than two small rooms. He preferred no basement at all.[58]

In the gallery, bookshelves constrict the space to a little more than three feet wide, but the clerestory relieves the closeness of the passage. Unlike the typical Usonian clerestory, with the window glass sandwiched between two perforated boards, the casements operate independently of the ornamental panels; Mrs. Hagan suggested the change to eliminate the chore of cleaning so many geometrically shaped areas of the glass.

More ample than the guest room, the middle bedroom also enjoys better light. A slight mistake was made at the south corner of the room, which comes to an acute angle; the stone jamb was squared to

Middle bedroom

accord with a carelessly drawn detail in the blueprints. "One square corner. . . . Mr. Hagan didn't like that," Jesse Wilson recalls. Another deviation from the unit lines occurs in the bathroom shared with the master bedroom. An angled partition designed to form one side of a toilet stall would have diverged sharply from the head of the bathtub, and the plumber refused to install a shower head that pointed water onto the bathroom floor. His common sense prevailed, the stall was omitted, and the partition was squared-off with the tub.

The last bedroom is also the largest, although part of its space is

Master bedroom, looking southwest

consumed by the extra linen closets and wardrobes Mrs. Hagan re-
quested along the west wall. She also wanted them carried up to the
deck, but Wright refused to interrupt the clerestory. The extra cases
are ventilated by small cutouts that repeat the basic figure of the floor
plan, the equilateral triangle.

Master bedroom, fireplace

An equilateral triangle also determines the shape of the chimney, which rises as a coda to the plan. It responds to the opposite salient, the acute angle of the great terrace prow. The house thus ends as it begins, lovingly settled into the hill known as Kentuck Knob.

AFTERWORD

As a late example of Frank Lloyd Wright's residential architecture, the house on Kentuck Knob occupies a special place by virtue of the beauty and isolation of its mountain site, the vitality of its plan, and the quality of its materials and construction.

Lord Palumbo's decision to open the house for regular tours allows a broad public to perceive more directly why Kentuck, from its inception, assumed such a large presence in the lives of the Hagans. For the house is obviously not an ordinary place in which to live; nor does its relatively small size in any way lessen its many surprises and charms.

Kentuck clearly belongs to a family of houses somewhat paradoxically conceived by Wright as more expensive and elegant developments of his prototype Usonian schemes of the Depression years. The purpose of the Usonian house was to provide the typical American family of modest income the chance to live in a relatively low-cost and system-built house with thin walls of wood, plenty of windows and glass doors, a flat but dramatically cantilevered roof, heat from pipes below a concrete floor mat, no basement, and a carport in place of a garage. The various plans were quite simple, and all the visible features were meant to encourage an expansive, high-spirited way of life in a country dedicated to freedom.

Despite this spareness in materials and details, the basic Usonian house expressed the fundamental principles and characteristics Wright had gradually evolved in the celebrated Prairie houses he designed during the first few years of the twentieth century.

For clients of greater means, however, Wright always stood ready to plan more substantial houses, with walls of brick or stone, often destined for much larger sites. His flair and talents were such that he could easily attract upper-middle-class and wealthy patrons.

Like so many other architects, Wright craved opportunities to design larger, more conspicuous buildings. His nonresidential commissions included such tours de force as the Unity Temple (1905–1908) in Oak Park, Illinois, the S. C. Johnson & Son Administration

Building (1936–1939) in Racine, Wisconsin, and the Price Tower (1952–1956) in Bartlesville, Oklahoma.

But his extraordinary ways of honoring the human scale throughout a building and thereby ennobling the lives of individuals meant that his residential work continued to form the very basis of his architecture, as the house on Kentuck Knob so wonderfully makes evident.

NOTES

1. Frank Lloyd Wright, *Modern Architecture: Being the Kahn Lectures for 1930* (Princeton, N.J., 1931), p. 65. Also see Frank Lloyd Wright, "In the Cause of Architecture: The Logic of the Plan," *Architectural Record* 63 (January 1928), p. 57.

2. The company offices were at the rear of 54 So. Gallatin Ave. Hagan's father, A. J. Hagan, had been president, but by 1953 was secretary-treasurer. I. N. Hagan was born in Uniontown in December 1907 and died there in January 1992. Bernardine Hagan was born in neighboring Somerset County in February 1909. Both attended two years of college.

3. A map published in London in 1753 identifies the ridges of Pennsylvania as the Endless Mountains. Fayette County was settled in the latter half of the eighteenth century, but not quickly; most of the Ohio River Valley was contested not only by the French and the British but also by Virginians and Pennsylvanians, and the Indians still regarded the land as their hunting grounds. Bituminous coal was discovered near Pittsburgh in

1759. The output from Pennsylvania reached its peak in 1918. See S. J. Buck and E. H. Buck, *The Planting of Civilization in Western Pennsylvania* (Pittsburgh, 1939), passim; Walter "Buzz" Storey, *Stories of Uniontown and Fayette County* (Uniontown, Pa., 1993), pp. 16–17, 214–15; "Fayette Co., Pa.," U.S. Geological Survey (Reston, Va., 1982); and James R. Shaulis, "Coal Resources of Fayette County, Pennsylvania," pt. 1 (Harrisburg, Pa., 1985).

4. Hagan wrote Wright about moving into the country on November 3, 1953. Ohiopyle, situated by spectacular waterfalls, dates from the eighteenth century and has been variously known as Pile City and Falls City. Indians named the Youghiogheny for its twisted course. It is the principal tributary of the Monongahela River, which joins the Allegheny River at Pittsburgh to form the great Ohio River. Fayette County, which glories in peaceful vistas, is named for the Marquis de Lafayette (1757–1834), a hero of the American Revolutionary War. The most famous native of Uniontown is Gen. George C. Marshall, (1880–1959), chief of staff of the American army during World War II.

5. *History of Fayette County, Pennsylvania,* ed. Franklin Ellis (Philadelphia, 1882), vol. 1, p. 775. The Kentuck District appears on the Stewart township map in the *Atlas of the County of Fayette and the State of Pennsylvania* (Philadelphia, 1872), plate 59. *Kentucke* is an Indian word of uncertain meaning. Kentuck Knob was part of a farm tract dating back to 1794. The first U.S. census, in 1790, found a population of 13,325 in Fayette County. Nearly half the settlers were of English origin. Chalk Hill is a diffuse village on U.S. 40, the route of the old National road, built from 1811 to 1818 as the first interstate highway.

6. Peles lived until January 1956, and his wife until March 1966. They paid $3,000 for the property on March 6, 1915. See the Fayette County deed record book 346, p. 79, and book 789, p. 384. The Hagans reforested the knoll by planting some 8,000 seedlings. The trees serve as a windbreak but also obscure the distant vistas one would expect from a mountain site.

7. Baker, now a New York architect, has more vivid memories of a much later visit to Bear Run. Snow was falling, it was Thanksgiving, and Edgar Kaufmann jr., who had inherited the house, was entertaining guests that included Ralph Kirkpatrick, the distinguished harpsichordist. Silas Paul Hagan was born in 1932 and died in 1989. See the *Princeton Weekly Bulletin,* February 21, 1990, p. 48, and the *Nassau Herald* [yearbook] (Princeton, 1954), p. 128.

8. See his senior thesis, "The Architecture of Frank Lloyd Wright and Le Corbusier" (1954), p. 66. Quoted by permission of the Princeton University libraries. Kaufmann (1885–1955) had a penchant for pranks and told Paul Hagan that Wright first designed for Bear Run a house suspended from cables over the stream and approached by electrically operated drawbridges. Paul Hagan duly wrote that Kaufmann remarked, "This was a bit too dramatic for me." Kaufmann once kept a dairy herd himself; see *The Friends of Fallingwater Newsletter* 15 (October 1996), pp. 1–6.

9. "The best thing to do is go as far out as you can get. Avoid the suburbs," Wright wrote in *The Natural House* (New York, 1954), p. 134.

10. Cotton, now a St. Louis architect, was especially interested in church architecture, and Mr. and Mrs. Hagan also took him to Saint Vincent Archabbey in Latrobe, Pa., where for the second annual Wimmer lecture,

in December 1948, Erwin Panofsky delivered his celebrated paper, "Gothic Architecture and Scholasticism." Cotton later wrote his senior thesis on Catholic church architecture.

11. Wright's reception of new clients is well described by John Sergeant in *Frank Lloyd Wright's Usonian Houses* (New York, 1976), p. 106. Mies van der Rohe, by contrast, in his later years was proud to say he did not hesitate to reject commissions that failed to interest him, or building programs for which "not God could find a solution." See the *Kansas City Times,* July 17, 1963, p. 26.

12. Curtis Besinger, in *Working with Mr. Wright* (Cambridge, England, 1995), p. 190, notes of the Meeting House that many of its construction details "were similar to those of the houses on which we were working."

13. Paul Hagan, senior thesis, pp. 15, 16, 27. Students at Princeton were forbidden to have cars, but he was vice-president of the "Princeton Sports Car Club" and kept a Jaguar XK-120 off campus.

14. The French and Indian War was a prelude to the world-wide war of 1756–1763 known as the Seven Years' War. Washington wrote of his "pallisado" fort, saying he had "prepar'd a charming field for an Encounter." The encounter took place on July 3, 1754, and proved to be the only occasion he was ever forced to surrender. See *The Writings of George Washington,* ed. John C. Fitzpatrick (Washington, D.C., 1931), pp. 54, 70.

15. Taliesin was built on the brow of a hill, and even the Hollyhock House (1916–1921) in Los Angeles, often considered an exception to Wright's dictum, leaves unencumbered the highest point of Olive Hill.

16. Howe (1913–1997) remained at Taliesin until September 1964. All

the sketches, dated February 1, and a revised plan of March 15 are now owned by Lord Palumbo. John Rattenbury and Bruce Brooks Pfeiffer, both apprentices at the time, attribute the sketches to Howe (except for some lettering) and the April 1954 working drawings to Allen L. Davison.

17. Wright, *The Natural House*, p. 165.

18. For the struggle with the museum, see *Frank Lloyd Wright: The Guggenheim Correspondence*, ed. Bruce Brooks Pfeiffer (Carbondale, Ill., 1986). The increasing work load at Taliesin is a recurrent theme in Besinger's memoir, *Working with Mr. Wright*. He writes (p. 225) that while some houses came almost completely from Wright, others were derived from earlier designs and still others were designed by senior apprentices, subject to Wright's changes.

John Geiger, an apprentice from 1947 to 1954, emphasizes the role of the apprentices in Wright's later work. "The last ten years of his life," he said recently, "he was very much involved with the Guggenheim—and that was his goal, to get that building built. A lot of other things fell by the wayside. By 1949 or 1950 he was very little involved in the houses except for special cases." In the *Journal of the Taliesin Fellows* 2 (fall 1990), pp. 13–15, Geiger tells of an occasion when Wright commented that sometimes a design issued from his studio "without benefit of clergy."

19. Even the plan published in *House & Home* 18 (September 1960), p. 118, mistakenly orients the house to the northwest. Mark Heyman, a Taliesin apprentice from 1954 to 1959, recently recalled Kentuck primarily because of the concern about its siting.

20. Wright, *The Natural House*, p. 150.

21. Wright, *Architectural Forum* 68 (January 1938), p. 68. He also wrote (p. 54) that the one-two triangle generated his 1928–1929 project for St. Mark's Tower in New York. The same project was reworked in 1952–1953 to become the Price Tower in Bartlesville, Okla.

22. Ibid., p. 64. Also see Edgar Kaufmann jr., *9 Commentaries on Frank Lloyd Wright* (New York, 1989), pp. 105–06.

23. "Mr. Wright would have blown his top if he'd seen that as the unit," Curtis Besinger said recently when shown copies of the working drawings for Kentuck. On the geometric basis of nature and architecture, see Wright, "In the Cause of Architecture: The Meaning of Materials—Stone," *Architectural Record* 63 (April 1928), p. 356, and *An Autobiography* (New York, 1943), p. 422. Wright dismissed imitative realism and literary representation as "subgeometric." He also disapproved of free-form architecture; when the architect Bruce Goff showed him photographs of buildings by Antoni Gaudí, he remarked, "I call that architecture with a laxative."

24. Besinger finds the unit dimension "unbelievable." Because the floor area of Kentuck subsumes about 950 of the triangles, each representing 332.25 square inches, the interior space can be estimated at about 2,200 square feet. The living room is by far the largest space, nearly three times larger than the master bedroom. Norman Tyler, in a valuable manuscript titled "Comparison Study of the I. N. Hagan House, Frank Lloyd Wright, Architect" (November 1983), at the Uniontown Public Library, takes the hexagon as the fundamental figure, while William Allin Storrer, in *The Frank Lloyd Wright Companion* (Chicago, 1993), p. 405, asserts that the unit is an equilateral parallelogram.

25. Wright, *A Testament* (New York, 1957), p. 220. Also see "In the Cause of Architecture: The Logic of the Plan," *Architectural Record* 63 (January 1928), p. 50. Floor mats served as the module for determining the rooms of traditional buildings in Japan and China.

26. Davison (1913–1974) was born in Edgewood, on the east side of Pittsburgh, and attended the Hill School in Pottstown, before he entered Cornell University in 1932. He graduated in 1937 with a bachelor's degree in architecture. After he refused to serve in World War II, he was imprisoned at Sandstone, Minn., where he perfected his skills at architectural rendering. "Davy is mastering color," Wright noted in January 1944. "And what beautiful renderings." See *Frank Lloyd Wright: Letters to Apprentices* (Fresno, Calif., 1982), p. 155.

27. For the office building design, see *Frank Lloyd Wright Monograph 1951–1959*, ed. Yukio Futagawa (Tokyo, 1988), p. 145. For the preliminary sketches Wright was charging 5 percent of the estimated construction costs of $50,000.

28. A phrase Wright had used in a letter of January 28, 1937, to Edgar Kaufmann jr. Hagan's letter about the final costs is dated October 7, 1957.

29. Interview with Louis Penfield, p. 4, in the Frank Lloyd Wright Archives (quoted by permission of the Frank Lloyd Wright Foundation). The State Theater, designed by Thomas Lamb of New York, opened on October 30, 1922. Keys (1881–1969) impressed Mrs. Hagan as a constant complainer: "He was such a contentious man, but he really knew what he was doing," she recalled in 1983. See Paul Wicke, "Wright Home Changed the Lives of Many," *Greensburg* [Pa.] *Tribune-Review,* January 30, 1983, p. 8.

30. "It's just like a dream," Wilson remarked when he returned to Kentuck in September 1997, at the age of eighty-eight. "I wore out three pairs of shoes stepping on the spalls. That was a back-breaking job." The stone weighs about 100 pounds per cubic foot, according to Wilson.

31. Edgar Tafel, *Apprentice to Genius* (New York, 1979), p. 90; also Wright, "The Eternal Law," in *Frank Lloyd Wright and Madison,* ed. Paul E. Sprague (Madison, Wis., 1990), p. 9. The Hagans had visited Edgar Kaufmann at his office in Pittsburgh, which Wright designed and which was paneled in cypress; see Christopher Wilk, *Frank Lloyd Wright: The Kaufmann Office* (London, 1993). Later, they visited the house Wright designed for his youngest son, Llewellyn Wright, in Bethesda, Md., and noted the damage suffered by its untreated cypress. The agents of decay are sunlight, moisture, and mildew. See Harvey E. Kennedy jr., "Baldcypress" (Washington, D.C., 1972), and Brad Lemley, "Swamp Wood," in *This Old House* (July/August 1997), pp. 40–44.

32. Coughenour (1886–1967) was active in the Asbury Methodist Church, as were Hagan and Eggers. Also see Wicke, "Wright Home Changed the Lives of Many," p. 8.

33. Wright, "In the Cause of Architecture: Sheet Metal and a Modern Instance," *Architectural Record* 64 (October 1928), pp. 334, 337. Bruce Herrington of Rector, Pa., who was a salesman for Williams & Co., of Pittsburgh, wholesalers of nonferrous metals, recalls selling the Revere sheet copper to Henry Cooper.

34. The description of Wright's visit to Kentuck appears in an interview with Mrs. Hagan by Richard Cleary and Robert S. Taylor on August 15,

1988. The date of Wright's visit remains uncertain. It must have been after Edgar J. Kaufmann died, in April 1955, because his son had invited Wright to Bear Run to discuss further building projects. Hagan wrote on May 11 that he looked forward to Wright's visiting the building site "reasonably soon."

35. *House Beautiful* 98 (November 1955), p. 336. Besinger, in *Working with Mr. Wright,* p. 280, remarks that Wright showed little interest in the designs for Heritage Henredon. Also see Christa C. Mayer Thurman, "'Make Designs to Your Heart's Content': The Frank Lloyd Wright/Schumacher Venture," in *The Prairie School* (Chicago, 1995) pp. 153–63.

36. Betsy Darrach, "Hans Wegner," *Interiors* 118 (February 1959), p. 84. An armchair and side chair of Wegner's design can be seen at Kentuck in James D. Van Trump, "Caught in a Hawk's Eye: The House of I. N. Hagan at Kentuck Knob," *Charette* (Pittsburgh), April 1964, p. 21. Edgar Kaufmann jr. (1910–1989) was known for his "Good Design" exhibits at the Museum of Modern Art.

37. Edgar Kaufmann jr., "Nakashima, American Craftsman," *Art in America* 43 (December 1955), pp. 30, 32. Hagan in 1970 ordered a special oak-burl dining table from Nakashima. The cypress table designed for the house was put in storage. The Hagans retained all the Nakashima pieces when they sold Kentuck in February 1986 to Lord Palumbo. The cypress table is now back in place.

38. George Nakashima, *The Soul of a Tree* (Tokyo, 1981), pp. 69, 215. Also see his sales catalogs, titled *George Nakashima, Woodworker.* Nakashima was born in 1905 in Spokane, Wash., and died in 1990. Edgar

Kaufmann jr., who had a Nakashima table in his Sutton Place apartment in New York, once remarked that Nakashima's free edges were not entirely compatible with Wright's geometrical order of design.

39. Wright, *An Autobiography,* p. 168.

40. Wright, in the *Architectural Forum* 68 (January 1938), p. 95. Because of the difficulties in siting the house, the prow rises more than four feet higher than shown in the working drawing of the northwest elevation. The prow brings to mind Wright's famous *Dampfer* (steamship) house (1908–1910) for Fred C. Robie in Chicago.

41. Wright, *An Autobiography,* p. 309. The roof was rebuilt after a fire on May 26, 1986, which began at the pump room and spread across the carports and into the bedrooms; see the *Herald-Standard,* May 27, 1986, pp. 11, 12, and May 28, pp. 1, 2. Much of the cypress paneling was replaced, and so was some of the stonework.

42. Wright, *An Autobiography,* p. 168. In *Architectural Forum* 68 (January 1938), p. 37, he wrote of "native stone rising from boulders of the same stone" in describing Fallingwater. He used random boulders in the lower walls of the Chauncey Williams house around 1895 in River Forest, Ill.

The walls of Kentuck up to floor-level are of stone veneer about ten inches thick; above that, double stone walls are separated by two inches of insulation. The preliminary sketches showed walls of flagstones combined with boulders, not a happy idea and not a good expression of the horizontal. The change to smaller stones in random ranges can be seen in the perspective sketch.

43. *Frank Lloyd Wright: Collected Writings,* ed. Bruce Brooks Pfeiffer,

vol. 3 (New York, 1993), p. 223. In *An Autobiography,* p. 171, Wright described the exterior walls of Taliesin as "an abstract combination of stone and wood as they naturally met in the aspect of the hills around." The stones of Kentuck expressed time and change, just as the copper roof aged to a verdigris and the exterior cypress—Wright thought—would be left to weather. The south wall is almost 120 feet long. In rock-structure pattern, Stewart township is composed of sequences of repetitive strata of shale, sandstone, red beds, limestone, and bituminous coal. Five old coal-mining sites lie south of Kentuck Knob along the branches of Cucumber Run.

44. Wright, *An Autobiography,* p. 349. Wright considered the "vanishing wall" a hallmark of his work and an expression of the American ideal of freedom. See his *Collected Writings,* vol. 2 (New York, 1992), pp. 95, 96.

45. Wright's notion of the dotted line was inspired by the Arizona desert; see *An Autobiography,* p. 309.

46. A one-to-four ratio of riser to tread was standard in Wright's studio. The risers at Kentuck, roughly four inches high, should be compared with ordinary steps of seven inches or more, Mark Heyman emphasizes. The Hagans rejected two earlier designs for the clerestory panels, which can be compared with the interior *ramma* of Japanese houses.

47. The working drawings show partition walls only two-and-a-half inches thick, Wright's standard detail, but they were built almost twice that width.

48. Wright, *The Natural House,* p 156. The height of the sloped ceiling is slightly more than ten vertical units; the outer dimension of each light box measures twelve inches, or half the height of the equilateral triangles

in the floor-plan grid. The built-in seat, twenty-eight feet long, encloses storage space. Cabinets at the far end of the seat were designed to hold a television set, radio, and phonograph.

49. Wright, "In the Cause of Architecture: The Meaning of Materials—Wood," *Architectural Record* 63 (May 1928), pp. 481, 486. One of the accomplishments of the Usonian houses, Wright thought, was the elimination of plastering. Wood ceilings became a feature of his houses in Los Angeles soon after he returned from Japan for the last time, in the summer of 1922.

50. Wright, *An Autobiography,* p. 347. "True ornament is the inherent melody of structure," he wrote in *Architectural Forum* 68 (January 1938), p. 100. The continuity of the indoor and outdoor planters should be compared with the moss garden at the second-story bridge over the drive at Fallingwater.

51. *Frank Lloyd Wright: Collected Writings,* vol. 5 (New York, 1995), pp. 79, 88; Wright, *The Natural House,* pp. 175, 176. Besinger, in *Working with Mr. Wright,* p. 287, notes that Wright was susceptible to drafts. Low light levels in Kentuck make the rooms appear cooler.

52. In either event, paradoxically, large areas of the floor were to be covered with carpets. Hagan objected to the "hog rods" in a letter of August 13, 1954, addressed to Davison rather than Wright. His letter about "natural stone" is dated September 26, 1955. The flagstones are laid in a random pattern, with wide mortar joints that meander like rivulets.

53. Terry L. Patterson, *Frank Lloyd Wright and the Meaning of Materials* (New York, 1994), p. 78, finds this detail a violation of "the structural nature of masonry."

54. Mrs. Hagan did not particularly like the high finish of the dining table and found it difficult to protect. The only other items of Wright's freestanding furniture that belong with the house are a veneered hexagonal table near the entry and a tall wooden weed holder, square in section, that he gave the Hagans.

55. Wright, *Architectural Forum* 68 (January 1938), p. 82. Significantly, it is the kitchen, not the hearth, that is perceived as the center and pivot point of the house. Its clutter, if any, is well hidden; yet the vistas from within prove much more attractive than one would expect from studying the floor plan.

56. All the cabinets and wardrobes at Kentuck have piano hinges. The stainless steel came from the Elkay Manufacturing Co. of Chicago, which had furnished the kitchen of the exhibition house on the Guggenheim Museum site. Mrs. Hagan omitted a maple cutting board, as well as an accordion screen of "hinged boards" between the kitchen and dining area. Eugene Masselink was commissioned later to design a four-panel folding screen decorated with an abstraction inspired by the angles of the floor plan. It was used in the master bedroom.

57. The partition behind the toilet deviates from the unit lines and forms a right angle.

58. Heating pipes above the basement had to be placed in the concrete floor slab. The furnace is oil fired, and the hot water is circulated by Bell and Gossett pumps. Twelve valves adjust the flow to various areas of the house. "It was a treat," Philip Cotton recalls of the heating system. "It was so pleasant, you wanted to sit on the floor in the winter."

Photo credits

All black and white photographs and diagrams are by the author unless otherwise noted in the caption. All color photographs are by Robert P. Ruschak.